SIMPLE MACHINES

PULLEYS ARE MACHINES

DOUGLAS BENDER

A Crabtree Roots Plus Book

CRABTREE
Publishing Company
www.crabtreebooks.com

T0011478

School-to-Home Support for Caregivers and Teachers

This book helps children grow by letting them practice reading. Here are a few guiding questions to help the reader with building his or her comprehension skills. Possible answers appear here in red.

Before Reading:

• What do I think this book is about?
  - *I think this book is about pulleys.*
  - *I think this book is about how important pulleys are in our everyday life.*

• What do I want to learn about this topic?
  - *I want to learn how pulleys work.*
  - *I want to learn how pulleys are used in different jobs.*

During Reading:

• I wonder why...
  - *I wonder why a rope and a wheel are parts of a pulley.*
  - *I wonder why a pulley is called a simple machine.*

• What have I learned so far?
  - *I have learned that pulleys help us move things.*
  - *I have learned that pulleys can be big or small.*

After Reading:

• What details did I learn about this topic?
  - *I have learned that a flagpole uses one small pulley to raise and lower the flag.*
  - *I have learned that elevators use many big pulleys.*

• Read the book again and look for the vocabulary words.
  - *I see the word **wheel** on page 9 and the word **elevators** on page 20. The other vocabulary words are found on page 23.*

This is a **pulley**.

Pulley

Lever

Screw

It is a **simple machine**. There are six simple machines.

Wedge

Inclined Plane

Wheel and Axle

A simple machine has few or no moving parts.

A pulley has two parts.

rope

A pulley has a **rope**.

wheel

The rope moves
along a **wheel**.

Pulleys help us move things. This pulley moves skiers up the mountain.

Sometimes people use more than one pulley.

Many pulleys help us move big things, such as a sail on a sailboat.

Pulleys can be small.

A **flagpole** uses
one small pulley.

Sam pulls the rope to raise the flag.

Pulleys can also be big.

Elevators use many big pulleys!

Word List
Sight Words

a	it	pulls
along	many	school
also	more	small
at	move	than
be	moves	the
big	moving	things
can	no	this
few	on	two
has	one	us
help	or	use
is	parts	uses

elevators

flagpole

pulley

rope

simple machine

wheel

CRABTREE
Publishing Company

SIMPLE MACHINES
PULLEYS
ARE MACHINES

Written by: Douglas Bender
Designed by: Rhea Wallace
Series Development: James Earley
Proofreader: Janine Deschenes
Production coordinator
 and Prepress technician: Katherine Berti
Print coordinator: Katherine Berti
Educational Consultant: Marie Lemke M.Ed.

Photographs:
Shutterstock: VDB: cover, p. 1; Nach Noth: p. 3, 23;
 Chris Lawrence Travel: p. 7, 23; Mikhail Gratkoskiy:
 p. 8, 9, 23; Konoplytska: p. 11; David Arosta Alley:
 p. 12-13; Cegli: p. 14; Juan Aunion: p. 15; Vibe
 Images: p. 17; Storman: p. 19; AvDe: p. 21, 23

Library and Archives Canada
Cataloguing in Publication

CIP available at Library and Archives Canada

Library of Congress
Cataloging-in-Publication Data

CIP available at Library of Congress

Crabtree Publishing Company

www.crabtreebooks.com   1-800-387-7650   Printed in the U.S.A./CG20210915/012022

Published in the United States
Crabtree Publishing
347 Fifth Avenue, Suite 1402-145
New York, NY, 10016

Published in Canada
Crabtree Publishing
616 Welland Ave.
St. Catharines, ON, L2M 5V6